GIRLS' SportsZone

GIRLS' SOCCER

By Brendan Flynn

SportsZone

An Imprint of Abdo Publishing
abdobooks.com

abdobooks.com

Published by Abdo Publishing, a division of ABDO, PO Box 398166, Minneapolis, Minnesota 55439. Copyright © 2022 by Abdo Consulting Group, Inc. International copyrights reserved in all countries. No part of this book may be reproduced in any form without written permission from the publisher. SportsZone™ is a trademark and logo of Abdo Publishing.

Printed in the United States of America, North Mankato, Minnesota.
102021
012022

Cover Photo: David Ribeiro/Alamy
Interior Photos: Steve Luciano/AP Images, 4–5; Alessandra Tarantino/AP Images, 7; Rich Grassle/Icon Sportswire, 10; Robin Alam/Icon Sportswire/AP Images, 12–13, 36–37; Leslie Plaza Johnson/Icon Sportswire/AP Images, 15; Andrea Vilchez/ SPP/Sipa USA/AP Images), 17; Francois Mori/AP Images, 18, 26; Alex Gallardo/ AP Images, 20–21; Remko Kool/Pro Shots/Sipa USA/AP Images, 23; Franck Fife/ AFP/Getty Images, 28–29; Matthew Visinsky/Icon Sportswire/AP Images, 31; Al Messerschmidt/Getty Images Sport/Getty Images, 32; David J. Philip/AP Images, 34; Laurent Cipriani/AP Images, 39; Jens Meyer/AP Images, 41; Shutterstock Images, 44

Editor: Charlie Beattie
Series Designer: Jake Nordby

Library of Congress Control Number: 2021941594

Publisher's Cataloging-in-Publication Data

Names: Flynn, Brendan, author.
Title: Girls' Soccer / by Brendan Flynn
Description: Minneapolis, Minnesota : Abdo Publishing, 2022 | Series: Girls' SportsZone | Includes online resources and index.
Identifiers: ISBN 9781532196362 (lib. bdg.) | ISBN 9781098218171 (ebook)
Subjects: LCSH: Soccer--Juvenile literature. | Sports for girls--Juvenile literature. | Soccer for girls--Juvenile literature. | Team sports--Juvenile literature.
Classification: DDC 796.334--dc23

TABLE OF CONTENTS

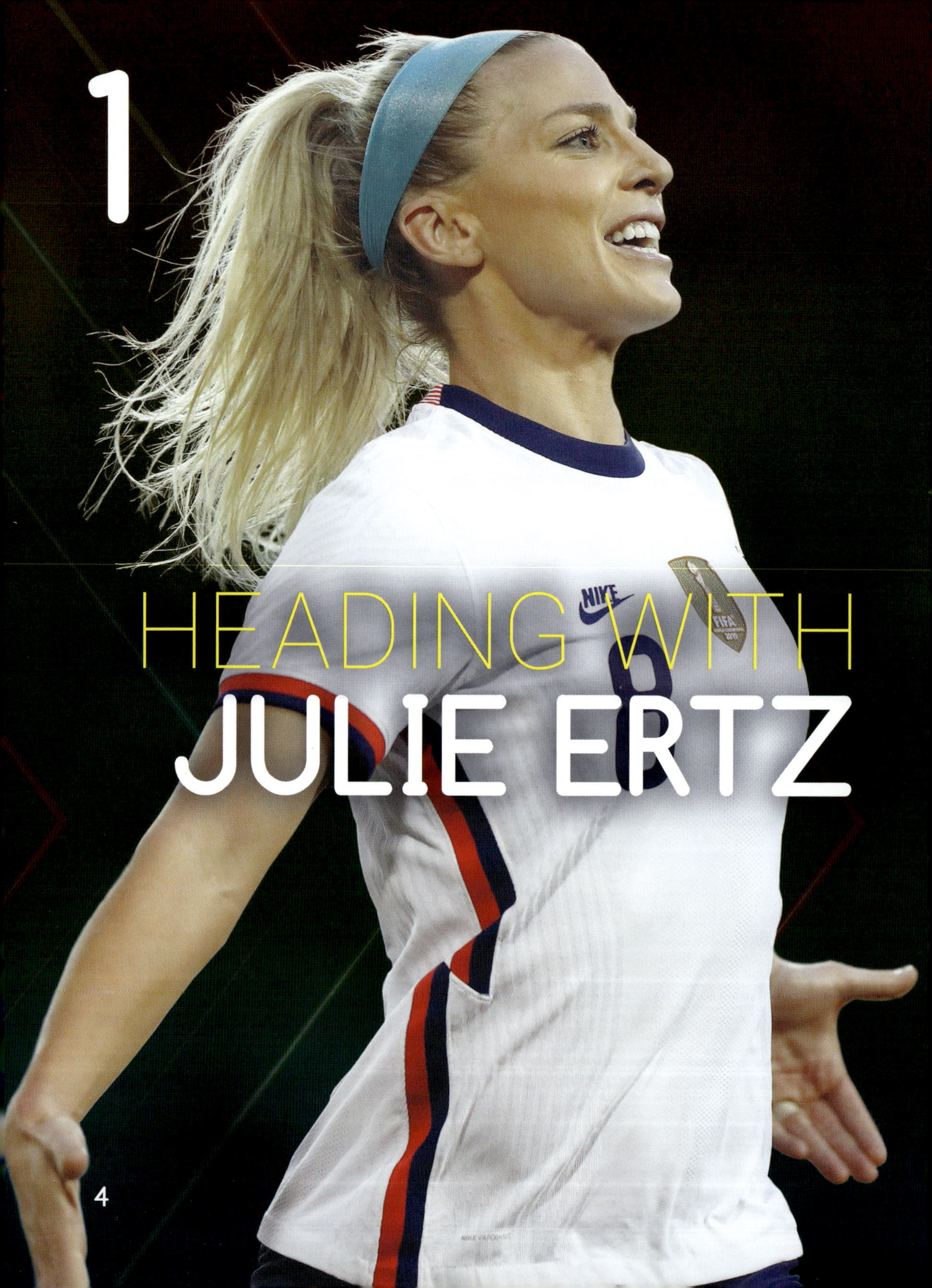
1
HEADING WITH
JULIE ERTZ

Set pieces are some of the most important plays in soccer. A set piece is any play that begins with a free kick or corner kick. When an attacking team has a set piece, players jostle for space near the goal as the ball is set. After the kick is taken, bodies crash into each other while players try to make a play.

That's when Julie Ertz is in her element. Ertz is a midfielder for the US Women's National Team (USWNT). She's a tough, skilled defender and a quality passer. But she also has a knack for getting her head to the ball on set pieces. And when she does, the ball often ends up in the back of the net.

Ertz's skills came in handy at the SheBelieves Cup in March 2020. The United States was locked in a scoreless battle with Spain in the 87th minute. A free kick was awarded just outside Spain's penalty area.

Forward Christen Press stepped up to take the kick. She served a low arcing ball into the box, just clearing the heads of two Spain defenders. Ertz timed her run perfectly, meeting the ball with her forehead. With a flick of her neck, she guided the ball past Spain's goalkeeper. The United States held on to win 1–0 and would eventually win the tournament.

Ertz has made a habit of scoring big goals, both for the USWNT and her club team, the Chicago Red Stars of the National Women's Soccer League (NWSL). Many of these goals have been memorable. In September 2017 she earned the NWSL Goal of the Week award when her diving header in the 84th minute lifted the Red Stars past the Carolina Courage 2–1.

A month later, playing for the USWNT against South Korea, Ertz headed home a corner kick from teammate Megan Rapinoe. That one also came on a dive, with the ball skipping between the shocked goalkeeper's legs. Those goals were a big reason Ertz was named the 2017 US Soccer Female Player of the Year.

Ertz celebrates after heading home the USWNT's second goal against Chile during the 2019 World Cup in France.

She won the award again in 2019 after scoring her most jaw-dropping header of all.

The USWNT was facing Chile in a 2019 Women's World Cup match. US defender Tierna Davidson sent a corner kick toward the center of the penalty area. Fighting for position, Ertz found herself facing away from the net. But this was no problem. She snapped her head backward, sending the ball on a line from the back of her head toward the top corner of the net. Chile's goalkeeper got both hands on the ball, but the shot was too powerful for her to handle.

Different Headers

Not all headers have the same purpose. A header shot needs to be hard and accurate. Usually, players will aim low with header shots. Shots that move from high to low are often harder for a keeper to save. So, a player should push her head forward and downward as she drives her forehead into the ball. Meanwhile, defensive headers are used to clear the ball away from danger. That means players often aim to hit the ball higher and farther. It is important for the defensive player to get under the ball. That way she can use her legs to help push upward and drive a powerful header away from goal.

The USWNT Twitter account called Ertz "our set piece queen" when it posted the highlight of her goal. She received even higher praise a year later, when USWNT head coach Vlatko Andonovski said Ertz "might be the most important player on this squad."

Honing the Header

Soccer is a game played primarily with the feet. However, field players can use other parts of their bodies, except for their hands and arms. The best players make plays with more than their feet. Often players trap or control the ball with their thighs or chest. Arguably the most important body part outside of the feet, however, is the head.

As Ertz has shown, headers are a great way to shoot on goal. A pass through the air is more effective when the penalty area is crowded. A header can then swiftly change the direction of the ball. That makes a well-placed shot off the head very difficult to save.

Defensive players also need to use their heads. A defensive header can quickly clear a cross or corner kick through the air. Players can also pass using headers. However, headers are more difficult to aim than a pass off a player's foot. The key for a headed pass is to send the ball to a teammate's feet. The feet are the best body part for controlling the ball.

Headers can also be dangerous. Proper technique is vital for preventing head and neck injuries. The first step is positioning. A player should bend her knees and position herself to squarely connect with the ball. Then she must properly hit the ball. Her eyes should be open so she can see the ball and time her header. And the header should always be purposeful. The ball should not simply bounce off one's head. Rather, the player should stiffen her neck and push her head into the ball. Certain parts of the head are safer and lead to more accurate passes. The forehead is always best to use, when possible. This helps aim the header while also preventing injuries, such as a concussion.

Ertz, *top*, jumps over Mexico's Lizbeth Ovalle during a May 2019 friendly match.

Getting to Ertz's level takes many hours of practice. It takes time to get used to hitting a fast-moving ball with your forehead. It takes even more time to learn to be accurate. But good headers are about more than technique. Positioning and size are also important. Many players who are good at heading are taller than their opponents. Their big frames allow them to get into good positions to meet the ball.

However, players do not have to be tall to be good at heading. Ertz proves that. She stands just 5 feet, 7 inches. That is about average for a women's soccer player. Any player can pass with her head in the open field. And with great instincts and positioning, even smaller players can be great shooters and defenders with their heads.

QUICK TIP:
HITTING THE SWEET SPOT

Former USWNT star Abby Wambach is among the greatest of all time at scoring with her head. Her coach with the national team, Pia Sundhage, knew what made Wambach's headers so successful. "She has power and timing, and she makes life very difficult for other teams," Sundhage said. Wambach learned from a young age through a specific drill. She would lie flat on her stomach while holding herself up with her elbows. Then she had someone sit in front of her and toss the ball toward her head. She would extend her neck forward, keeping her eyes looking straight ahead. Then she would meet the ball with her forehead and send it back to the person that tossed it. Wambach made sure to keep her neck strong and straight, rather than nodding her head up and down. The drill helps with timing the header and contacting the ball with the forehead rather than the top of the head.

2

SHOOTING WITH
**ALEX
MORGAN**

Alex Morgan stood on the cusp of history in April 2019. The 29-year-old striker had scored 99 goals for the USWNT, and she was eager to become the seventh US player ever to reach 100.

On April 4, against Australia, she made it happen. It was an international friendly, preparing both teams for the upcoming Women's World Cup. Morgan had scored her ninety-ninth goal against Japan five weeks earlier. But she was held scoreless in the next two matches. In the 14th minute, Morgan chased down a long clearing pass on the left side of the attacking zone.

First she used her strength to outmuscle an Australian defender for the ball. Then she dribbled toward the top of the penalty area and faked to her left, fooling a second defender. Morgan found herself with only the goalkeeper to beat. She did what she does best. She picked out a corner of the net, put her laces

Alex Morgan fires home her 100th international goal on April 4, 2019, against Australia.

Super Substitute

It might be hard to believe that Alex Morgan was ever a reserve player. But that is exactly what she was for much of her early career with the USWNT. Morgan's first international appearance was as a substitute against Mexico on March 31, 2010. She went on to play in seven more games for the USWNT that year. Every time, she came off the bench. Even at the 2011 Women's World Cup, when she scored in the semifinals and the final match, Morgan came in as a sub in all five of her appearances. She finally broke into the starting lineup for good in 2012 and played a key role as the United States won the next two Women's World Cups.

through the ball, and blasted home her landmark goal.

But Morgan was far from finished. Later that summer she tied a Women's World Cup record by scoring five goals in one match against Thailand. She then added a game-winning goal against England in the semifinals. Her six total goals were tied for the most in the tournament.

Morgan has consistently scored goals for the USWNT since her debut with the squad in 2010. She relies on a deadly shot to finish off attacks. She also puts herself in position to score through her tireless effort on the field. Morgan's determination and creativity help her put her elite shooting skills to good use. She has a knack for getting open and where she needs to be to receive a setup pass.

Morgan (13) scores with a volley against Trinidad and Tobago during a 2019 Olympic qualifying match.

"She's very difficult to deal with, obviously," longtime teammate Megan Rapinoe said. "She's a very willing runner, always in and around the goal box. Clinical finisher. She's always trying to sniff out to put herself in the best position to be in the goal box. When we get in there, we really have a good point of play as a team and provide a lot of service for her. She's always there, ready, and willing to be there."

Going for the Goal

Most goals are scored off a shot from a player's foot. For players like Morgan, their feet can score goals with multiple kinds of shots. As she showed against Australia, players often need to create the space to shoot. In that match, Morgan used her dribbling skills to split the defense. That left her one-on-one with the goalkeeper and gave her time to prepare her shot.

No matter how or from where, there are some fundamentals of shooting. Balance and positioning are key elements in setting up a shot. A player shooting with her right foot should try to plant her left foot next to the ball. That sets a balanced foundation so the right leg can swing powerfully through the ball. It is also important for the shooter to face her target. This helps a shot be more accurate.

Once a player has space to shoot, she must decide how hard to strike the ball. The most powerful shots come off the laces of a player's shoes. The harder the shot, the faster the keeper must react. However, powerful shots can also be harder to control. Sometimes a player might have a lot of

Birthday Brilliance

On July 2, 2019, Alex Morgan made history when she became the first woman to score a Women's World Cup goal on her birthday. She celebrated her thirtieth birthday by heading home a pass from Lindsay Horan in the first half of the semifinal against England. Morgan's goal proved to be the winner in a tight 2–1 victory.

Brazilian legend Marta lines up a penalty against Argentina during the 2021 SheBelieves Cup.

time and space to shoot. In that case, the key may be a softer but more accurate shot. Other times a goalkeeper might move farther out from the goal line. Then a player can try chipping the ball over the keeper's head with a soft, looping shot.

Rose Lavelle, *right*, splits two defenders to score for the USWNT in the 2019 World Cup Final against the Netherlands.

Placement is the other key factor in shooting. A player has the option of sending the ball high, low, left, right, or straight ahead. The best option often depends on the placement of both the shooter and the goalkeeper. A shot from the middle of the field offers more possibilities. Usually, the keeper will be standing in the middle of the net. So the best shot is often toward one of the corners.

It is harder to score when shooting from an angle. The keeper can move to one side and cut off more of the net. That leaves a smaller target at which to shoot. Against Australia, Morgan shot toward the far post. There is almost always more space to shoot on the wide side of the net.

Scoring on a breakaway requires skill and concentration. One way that players increase their chances is by shooting low. Goalkeepers make many saves with their hands. At close range, higher shots are often easier to save than low ones.

QUICK TIP:
STRAIGHT SHOOTING

One shot that all great strikers practice thousands of times is a low, hard drive. Alex Morgan is a left-footed player. When she approaches the ball, she faces her target and plants her right foot beside the ball. Morgan keeps her knee over the ball and leans her body forward. Her eyes look at the ball the whole time. Morgan dips her foot down to strike the ball with the laces. "That's where you're going to get the most power and the most accuracy," she says. "Typically, you want to follow through with that same striking foot and land on the same foot you kicked with."

3

DRIBBLING WITH TOBIN HEATH

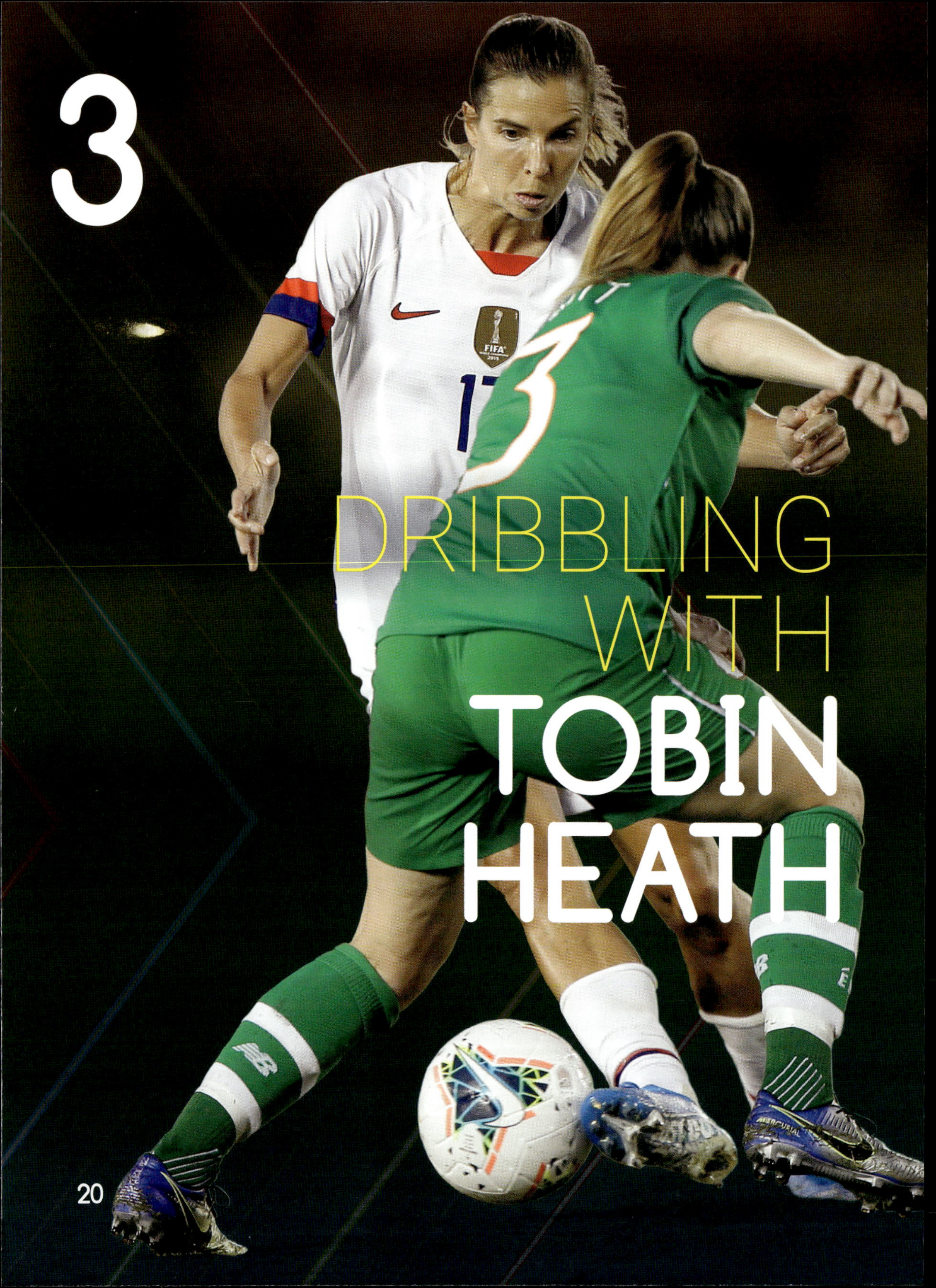

Everyone in the stadium pays attention when the ball is at Tobin Heath's feet. The crowd holds its collective breath. Defenders tense up. Her teammates anticipate something incredible, because that's what Heath can deliver on the field.

The winger's magical dribbling skills were on display at the 2018 Tournament of Nations. The USWNT was facing Brazil. Heath tracked down a pass on the far right near Brazil's penalty area. As she dribbled the ball into the box, two defenders backed up. They knew if they pressured Heath, they risked falling victim to her trademark move, the nutmeg—passing the ball between an opponent's legs. It is one of soccer's most humiliating moments for a defender.

Finally, one defender closed in. Heath stopped her momentum and stepped over the ball, first to the right, then back to the left. The first defender staggered backward,

Tobin Heath (in white) makes a move against Ireland during a 2019 friendly match.

not sure which way Heath was going. The second defender charged to Heath's left.

That was exactly what Heath wanted to happen. She tapped the ball to her right, giving her enough space to send a crossing pass in front of the Brazil net. Teammate Julie Ertz crashed toward the far post and slid, meeting the ball on a short hop and sending it into the net.

It was the kind of play Heath makes look routine. But soccer fans around the world know her skills with the ball are anything but common. The Internet is filled with highlight videos of Heath's most audacious moves. Sometimes she juggles the ball to flick it over a defender's head. Other times she deftly pokes a ball away from an opponent and passes it to a teammate with her heel. Still other times, she sends a defender sprawling with a devastating cutback move. In all cases, Heath's dribbling skills are legendary.

"I want to be an entertainer on the field, because that's

Getting Noticed

Heath, *left*, takes on a defender in a 2020 friendly match against the Netherlands.

what I enjoy watching," Heath said. "Players that kind of do things a little bit different, that can impact the game in a special way."

Heath's incredible ball skills didn't come out of nowhere. When she was around 10 years old, she was fortunate enough to play for a youth coach named Tom Anderson. He decided he would rather have his players improve and have fun than try to win every game. Anderson's vision helped nurture Heath's creativity. Her talent took over from there.

"I think we should be rolling the ball out there and letting them play and encouraging them to do every trick they see [from] Messi, Ronaldo, or any other—Neymar," said Anderson, citing some of the biggest stars in the game. "Any skill they see them do, they should be trying."

It is a lesson that Heath certainly took to heart.

Keeping the Ball

Dribbling is one of the most important parts of soccer. Besides passing, it is the main way the ball is moved around the field. A good touch on the ball can be the difference between beating a defender and losing the ball. It also can be the difference between creating a goal-scoring opportunity and a turnover.

To dribble a soccer ball is to control it. This is done through a series of light touches on the ball using the feet. However, dribbling can look different depending on the situation.

A player sprinting down the field with the ball will tap the ball slightly harder in front of her. The key is to keep control of the ball. If the player taps the ball too hard, it becomes easier to steal. If she taps it too softly, the player will have to slow down or risk losing the ball.

Dribbling in tight spaces often involves more touches. It is important for the dribbler to keep the ball close. If it sits farther away, it is harder for the person dribbling to control and easier for an opposing player to steal from the dribbler. That control becomes even more important when a defender gets close. The player with the ball needs to constantly keep the ball moving. If she does not, the defender can easily knock it away.

A player can dribble to hold on to the ball between passes. Players can also dribble to challenge defenders. The key to this is in a player's footwork. A good dribbler can keep the defender off balance by mixing things up. This can mean tapping the ball with different parts of her feet. Or she can tap the ball at different speeds. For example, a player might tap the ball three times softly and then tap it harder when making her move. But maintaining control is always the key.

More than Dribbling

Tobin Heath realizes she is known more for her dribbling skills than anything else. But she also enjoys using those skills to beat her opponents, in both one-on-one matchups and on the scoreboard. "There's a very strong duality to my game," Heath said. "I'm very creative, intuitive—I like to entertain. [But there is also] an intense desire to win, and to be effective, and to do whatever it takes."

Heath, *left*, shields the ball from French defender Elise Bussaglia during the 2019 World Cup quarterfinals.

Foot control is the most important part of dribbling. However, players such as Heath often use their bodies to try to confuse defenders. For example, a player might lower her left shoulder so the defender commits to that side. Then she will tap the ball harder to her right and break that way.

No one is born a great dribbler. The best players are constantly practicing and trying new moves. They often practice alone and find fun and creative ways to play with a soccer ball.

QUICK TIP:
CONING YOUR SKILLS

It takes a lot of practice to control the ball like Tobin Heath. One of the best ways to develop quality dribbling skills is to set up cones in various formations and dribble around them. Start off easy. Set up four to five cones in a straight line, each three giant steps apart from each other. Then dribble through them using both the outside and inside of your dominant foot. Try not to let the ball hit the cones. As you get more comfortable, switch feet. You can move the cones closer together to increase the difficulty.

4

PASSING WITH
MEGAN RAPINOE

The fun-loving Megan Rapinoe knows how to stand out. The USWNT star is hard to miss with her bleached-blond hair (which she sometimes dyes pink or purple). Her goal celebration against France in the 2019 World Cup has become an iconic twenty-first–century sports image. And she has made headlines with her activism focused on social justice issues, including equal pay for female athletes.

Behind all that is one of the most creative offensive players in the world. Rapinoe has an eye for the whole field and what is about to happen. Then she has the skills to get the ball to the perfect spot so the play can continue.

Rapinoe, a forward, has taken on more of a scoring role as she has become one of the USWNT's veteran players. But she has been on the delivery end of some of the most famous goals in US soccer history. It was Rapinoe who hit the long cross that Abby Wambach headed in to tie Brazil in the final moments of the 2011

Women's World Cup quarterfinals. It was Rapinoe who hit the long pass up the middle that Alex Morgan used to score the opening goal against Japan in the final. And it was Rapinoe who sent a cross flying through the night sky in the dying moments of the 2012 Olympic semifinal against Canada. Wambach finished that one as well, and the USWNT went on to win.

ACL Agony

Megan Rapinoe was rising through the ranks of the US women's soccer program in 2006 when she suffered an anterior cruciate ligament (ACL) injury. That forced her to have surgery on her knee. She had to regain her strength and ability to cut back and forth. Rapinoe was almost back to full health in 2007 when she reinjured her ACL. The second injury started the long recovery process all over again. She never gave up. Soon Rapinoe was one of the most valuable players on the USWNT.

"Megan, she's one of the players on our team that has the ability to change the game," Wambach said. "She can come on and be the best player on the field."

Rapinoe showed in a 2021 SheBelieves Cup match against Argentina that her passing touch has remained sharp despite her newfound scoring role. Already leading 2–0 on a pair of Rapinoe goals early in the first half, the United States kept up the pressure. In the 35th minute, US defender Tierna Davidson sent a long pass from just past the center line toward

Rapinoe on the left side of the field. Instead of settling the ball and turning to face the goal, Rapinoe quickly flicked it down the left side of the penalty area where teammate Kristie Mewis was making a run. Mewis tracked down the ball and passed it back to the center of the box where Carli Lloyd was waiting to send it into the net.

The play would not have happened if Rapinoe had not exhibited three very important traits for an elite passer. First she had the vision to know where Mewis would be heading.

Mia Hamm's vision and skill made her one of the best passers in soccer history.

She had the creativity to make a clever pass. And she was unselfish enough to set up her teammate, rather than trying to create her own shot.

Those skills helped make Rapinoe a key contributor to the USWNT early in her career. And they were still on display long after she had become the face of US women's soccer.

The Perks of Passing

Passing is the most efficient way to move the ball around the field. Any good soccer team must be able to string several consecutive passes together. A team that dribbles too much usually struggles to maintain possession. Passing serves many purposes in soccer. One is simply to keep possession of the ball. If defenders are pressuring a player, she can simply pass to an open teammate. That creates more time and space to eventually develop an attack. Maintaining possession often means passing to the sides and even to the back. The objective is simply to keep the ball safe and away from the other team until an attack can be built.

Every team must attack at some point. Passing is usually the best way to set up an attack. Players without the ball in soccer should always be moving to an open space. When attacking, the player with the ball often passes between two defenders to an area where a teammate is running. This is called a through ball. These types of passes take advantage of holes in the defense and can lead to scoring opportunities. "I've never scored a goal without receiving a pass from my

Amassing Assists

Forward Mia Hamm retired in 2004 with a record 158 career goals, a mark later broken by Abby Wambach. One record Hamm still holds is career assists. She racked up 144 in her career. Her best year was 2004, when she had 22.

teammates," said Wambach, the leading goal scorer in USWNT history, with 184.

Rapinoe has shown that there are many ways to get the ball to a teammate. The most common way to pass is with the inside of the foot. One foot is placed next to the ball and aimed toward the target. The other foot swings and sends the ball moving. Passes also can go through the air. These passes go farther. But they are less accurate and harder to receive. Most of these passes are made with the laces of a player's shoe. This is how most players take free kicks and corner kicks.

Fundamentals are important. But what sets players like Rapinoe apart is vision. Rapinoe watches her teammates. She can see where they are running and where there is open space. She knows exactly when and where to send the ball. As she has proven many times, that is a recipe for success.

QUICK TIP:
STAYING ON TARGET

Passing is only effective if it goes to the right place, whether that's to a teammate or to an open space. There are lots of ways you can work on passing accuracy. One simple drill requires a partner and some cones. Set two cones a few feet apart, making a "window." Stand back-to-back with your partner in the window and then take a few steps apart. Turn around, and the window should be between you and your partner. Try passing the ball through the cones and to your partner. Then she passes it back. If you're doing well, try standing farther apart or putting the cones closer together.

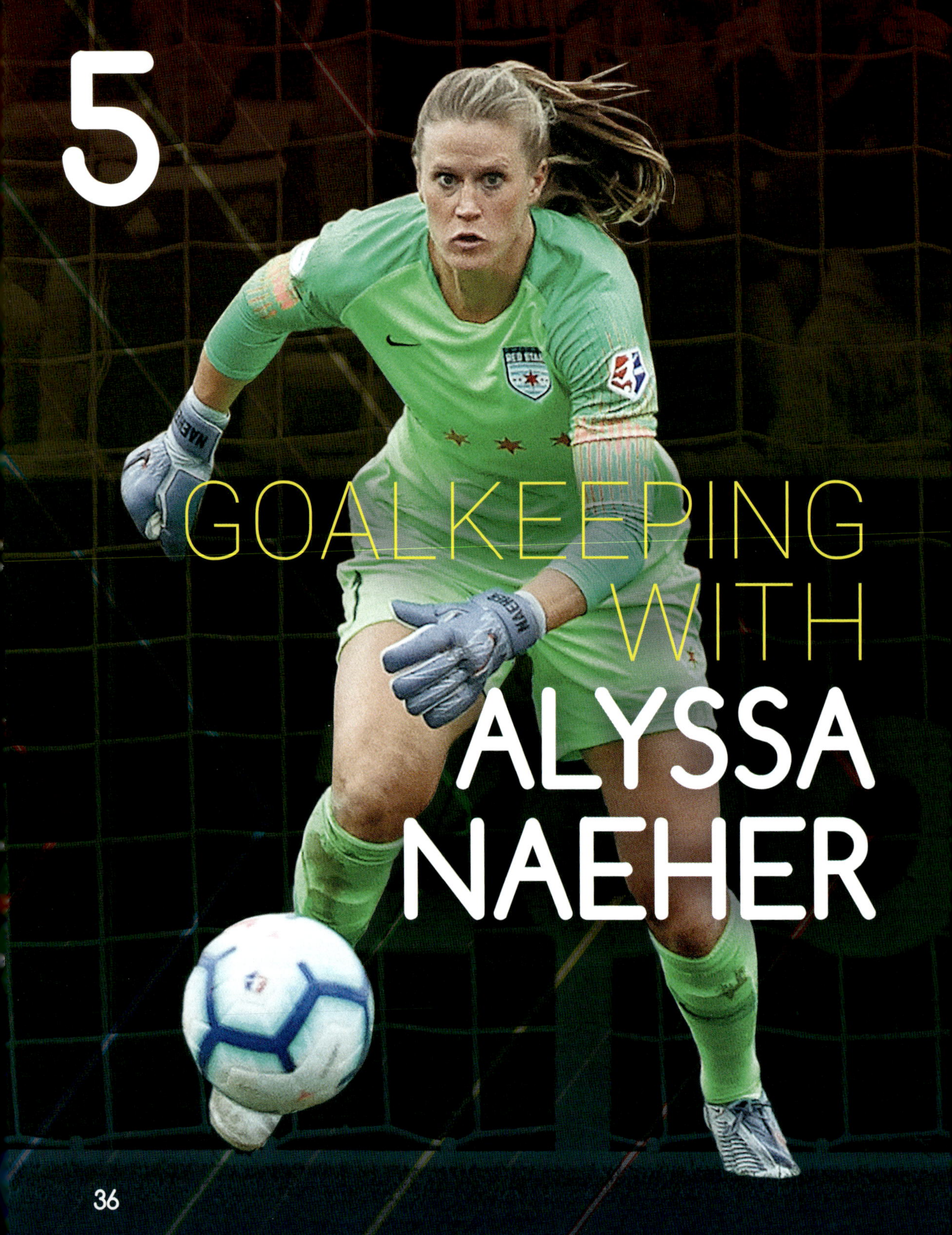

5
GOALKEEPING WITH ALYSSA NAEHER

Alyssa Naeher had big shoes to fill. Former USWNT goalkeeper Hope Solo was one of the greatest in the history of the game. Solo was the team's main keeper from 2005 to 2016. She led the team to two Olympic gold medals. Solo allowed just three goals in seven games as the United States won the Women's World Cup in 2015. After she retired, someone had to step up to take her place. That someone was Naeher.

After serving as one of Solo's backups since she joined the USWNT in 2014, Naeher slowly distanced herself from her competition to become the team's number one keeper after Solo's retirement.

However, she had not been tested in a big tournament yet. Solo played every minute of the 2015 Women's World Cup and did the same in the 2016 Olympics. Now all eyes were on Naeher as the team headed to France in the summer of 2019 to defend its Women's World Cup title.

Chicago Red Stars goalkeeper Alyssa Naeher charges after a ball during a July 2019 NWSL match.

Finding a Home

The keeper position is unique in soccer. Not everyone likes playing it. But Alyssa Naeher knew from early on that she was different. "I always liked it even when I was a kid," Naeher said. "I remember being at a soccer camp one summer when I was 12 years old, and I was going to split it up and take part in goalkeeper camp for half of the time and field player camp for the other half. I remember leaving my first goalkeeper camp session and I told my parents, 'You can take me out of the field player one, I'm a goalkeeper.'"

Naeher's teammates were fully confident in her abilities. "No one's given her time yet," said US midfielder Julie Ertz, who was also Naeher's teammate with the NWSL's Chicago Red Stars. "We know who she is. We train with her every day. We know how good she is. She's really good. Great with her feet, great shot stopper."

Naeher got off to a good start with three straight shutouts to begin the tournament. She then made four key second-half saves in a 2-1 quarterfinal win over France.

In the semifinals against England, Naeher got a chance to prove her teammates' confidence was not misplaced. The United States led 2–1 in the 83rd minute when defender Becky Sauerbrunn was called for a foul in the penalty area. England captain Steph Houghton stepped up to take the penalty kick.

Naeher, *right*, turns away Steph Houghton of England's penalty in the 2019 World Cup semifinals.

Naeher had only faced one penalty kick in her USWNT career, and she didn't stop it. She was also 0-for-7 in stopping penalties in her club career. But she later said she wasn't worried about Houghton scoring. "I felt pretty good going into it," Naeher said. "I just for some reason did not feel like she was going to score. I could feel that calmness from the whole team."

Naeher planted her heels on the goal line as she awaited Houghton's approach. The shot went low and to her right. Naeher read Houghton's shot, dived, and smothered the ball. She prevented not only a goal but a potential rebound as well.

As her teammates mobbed her, she quickly urged them to refocus and protect the lead for the rest of the game, which they did. Five days later, the USWNT clinched a second consecutive Women's World Cup title after a 2–0 victory over the Netherlands. Naeher had proved she could do what many had thought she could not—replace Solo. In the process, she had matched Solo's performance of 2015, allowing just three goals in seven matches.

Unbeatable

Fans might have thought Naeher was an overnight sensation, coming out of nowhere to save the day. But USWNT insiders knew otherwise. US goalkeeper coach Philip Poole was asked about Naeher's big save against England. His response could have applied to her performance the whole tournament: "It wasn't a coincidence. Lightning didn't strike. She's been ready for that. It was a culmination of her

Hope Solo stops a penalty against Brazil in the 2011 World Cup. Solo appeared 202 times for the USWNT from 2000 to 2016.

hard work, her mindset, and her professionalism all coming together on the same day."

Guarding the Goal

The goalkeeper has an important role. She is the last line of defense on any soccer team. It is her job to stop shots any way she can. Unlike field players, that includes stopping the ball with her hands and arms.

The casual fan might not notice everything that goes into a big save. First there is positioning. A keeper can cut off the shooter's angle by moving toward one post or the other. She can also do so by moving out toward an attacker. Once in position, the goalkeeper prepares herself for the shot. She gets low and stays light on her feet. That allows her to react immediately when the ball is kicked.

A keeper will often need to dive to stop shots. And she must decide how to stop the ball while diving. If she thinks she can stop the shot and catch it, diving with two hands is the only option. It is important for a goalkeeper to keep her hands together. This will give her the best chance of holding

QUICK TIP:
REACHING NEW HEIGHTS

Alyssa Naeher worked hard to achieve her excellent range. One of the drills a keeper can do to increase vertical jump height and improve reaction time and hand-eye coordination is called a "depth jump with ball." The keeper begins by standing on a box approximately 2 feet (0.61 m) off the ground. She steps off the box, landing with her feet shoulder-width apart and her toes pointed forward. As she hits the ground, a person standing a few feet in front of her tosses a ball in the air over her head. The goalkeeper immediately explodes off the ground and taps the ball back to the thrower.

the ball and preventing a rebound. If the shot is too far to catch, she might reach with just one hand and tip it over or around the goal.

It takes lots of practice to make technically sound saves. Decision-making and reaction speed are both important. Goalkeepers need to know exactly when to start a dive or to charge a player on a breakaway. Of course, keepers also need to have great athleticism to spring through the air and make a save.

Big saves make the postgame highlight reels. But there is so much more that goes into goalkeeping for an entire game. Goalkeepers also must be leaders of the defense. Since the keeper is in the back, she usually has the best view of the field. She takes charge of directing her teammates to cover open areas or find unmarked players.

Goalkeepers can also be important on offense. Any time a keeper makes a save and holds on to the ball, the possession changes. She then becomes the first move in a counterattack. A quick roll or throw to an open teammate can catch the opponents before they are set up defensively. But this also runs the risk of giving the ball right back to the other team. The goalkeeper may want to hold the ball and let her teammates move up the field for a longer punt. Whatever she decides often sets the tone for a counterattack.

FIELD
DIAGRAM

CORNER ARC
The spot from which a corner kick must be taken.

PENALTY SPOT
The point from which a penalty shot must be taken.

CENTER CIRCLE
Kickoffs take place in the center of this area. Only two players from the kicking team can be in the center circle during a kickoff.

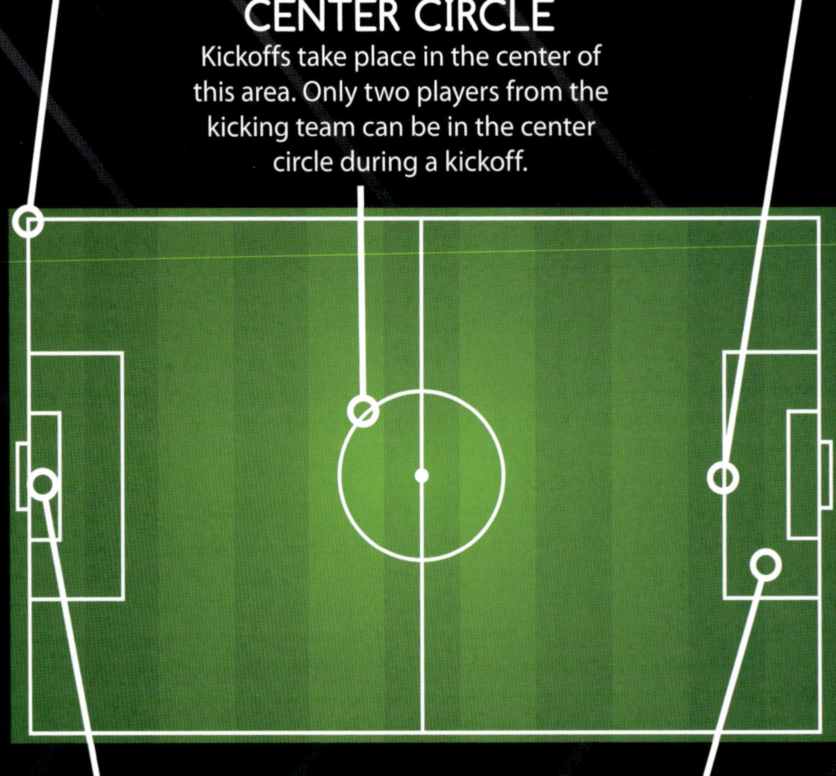

GOAL AREA
The area from which a goal kick must be taken.

PENALTY AREA
The area of the field in which goalkeepers can use their hands. It is also called the 18-yard box.

GLOSSARY

assist
A pass that leads directly to a goal.

audacious
Bold or daring.

corner kick
A free kick from a corner of the field near the opponent's goal.

counterattack
Quickly changing from defense to offense.

dribbling
Controlling and advancing the ball up the field with one's feet.

efficient
Taking less time and effort.

free kick
An unguarded kick awarded to a team after an opponent's foul.

momentum
The strength or force that allows something to continue or to grow stronger.

plant
To put a foot firmly on the ground.

rebound
When the ball bounces off something, usually a goalkeeper, to produce another scoring chance for the offense.

save
To stop the ball from going in the goal.

through ball
A pass between defenders to an open space where a teammate will soon be.

MORE INFORMATION

BOOKS

Carothers, Thomas. *Women's World Cup Heroes*. Minneapolis, MN: Abdo Publishing, 2019.

Marquardt, Meg. *STEM in the World Cup*. Minneapolis, MN: Abdo Publishing, 2020.

Marthaler, Jon. *US Women's Professional Soccer*. Minneapolis, MN: Abdo Publishing, 2019.

ONLINE RESOURCES

To learn more about women's soccer, please visit **abdobooklinks.com** or scan this QR code. These links are routinely monitored and updated to provide the most current information available.

PLACES TO VISIT

National Soccer Hall of Fame

9200 World Cup Way
Frisco, TX 75033
nationalsoccerhof.com

Learn the history of soccer in the United States, including its best moments and great players. The facility is located inside Toyota Stadium, the home of FC Dallas of Major League Soccer.

National Sports Center

1700 105th Ave. NE
Blaine, MN 55449
800-535-4730
nscsports.org

With 52 fields, the National Sports Center is recognized as the largest soccer complex in the world. Many youth soccer games and tournaments take place here each year, notably the USA Cup, which is considered the largest youth soccer tournament in the western hemisphere.

INDEX

ABOUT THE AUTHOR

Brendan Flynn is a San Francisco resident and an author of numerous children's books.